Stock Market Mastery
Strategies for Building Wealth

Table of Contents

Chapter 1. Introduction

Welcome to our enlightening Special Report: "Stock Market Mastery: Strategies for Building Wealth." Journey with us as we peel back the complex layers of the stock market to reveal practical, proven strategies that can help everyday individuals like you amass a fortune with time. Don't be held back any more by financial jargon and market intricacies. This report will empower you to step boldly into the world of stock investing and achieve your dreams of financial independence. With every page, imagine yourself unlocking the secrets of the wealthy and soon, being one of them. Get ready for a transformative journey that marries knowledge and financial success, setting you on your very own path to stock market mastery. You're just one step away from a better, richer future. Dive in with us now, as we confidently navigate the financial seas towards wealth and prosperity!

Chapter 2. Understanding the Stock Market: A Comprehensive Overview

The stock market, an intricate global network that plays a crucial role in international finance, is a daunting concept to many. Let's strive to strip away the complexities and get down to the basic principles that drive the stock market.

In very simple terms, a stock market functions as a marketplace for buyers and sellers of shares, or shares in public companies. These shares represent ownership in a company and investing in these can bring about significant financial reward if approached correctly.

2.1. The History of Stock Markets

The first recorded stock market exchange was established in the 17th century by the Dutch East India Company, making it possible for investors to buy ownership stakes in the company. This phenomenon quickly spread across Europe, with the London Stock Exchange being established in the late 18th century, followed by the New York Stock Exchange in the 19th century. So developed the modern concept of a centralized place where shares could be bought and sold.

2.2. Understanding Shares and Their Value

When you purchase a share, you're buying a tiny portion of a company, giving you a claim to a slice of the company's future earnings and assets. The value of a share can fluctitate drastically, determined by the supply-demand dynamics in the market. If a company performs well and is expected to continue on this path, the value of the stock increases. Conversely, poor company performance can lead to a decrease in stock value.

2.3. Different Types of Stocks

Stocks are often categorized into different types. There's 'Common Stock', the type most investors refer to when they talk about stocks. Holders of common stocks often have voting rights in the company. Then there's 'Preferred Stock', where the owners are assured a fixed dividend forever. If a company goes bankrupt, preferred stockholders have a higher claim on any remaining assets than common stockholders do.

Another way to distinguish between stocks is through 'Market Capitalization'. This is a company's total market value that is being traded on the stock market. Generally, companies are classified as small-cap, mid-cap, or large-cap companies, depending on their market value.

There're further classifications as 'Growth Stocks', companies that reinvest their earnings into expanding the business rather than paying dividends, and 'Dividend aka yield stocks', companies that reward shareholders by giving back a portion of their profits through dividends.

2.4. How Stock Markets Work

Stock markets function on the simple principle of supply and demand. An exchange provides a venue where stocks can be bought and sold. The price for each stock is determined by the market participants themselves.

When you decide to buy shares in a company, your broker communicates with the exchange, finds a seller, negotiates a price, and facilitates the transaction. Sophisticated computer systems keep track of these millions of trades happening each day.

2.5. Identifying Opportunities in Stock Market

One of the keys to stock market mastery is understanding how to identify opportunities. This requires an understanding of key indicators and analysis techniques.

One common form of analysis is 'Fundamental Analysis'. This involves reviewing a company's financial statements, assessing its management, understanding its competitive advantages, and more, aiming at determining a stock's intrinsic value.

Then there's 'Technical Analysis'. This involves looking at the stock's chart patterns, trends, and other statistical data to identify trading opportunities based on market participants' behavior.

Lastly, there are 'Economic Indicators' such as GDP, unemployment rate, inflation rate, and more, which give a comprehensive overview of the overall health of the economy and potential effects on certain sectors or companies.

2.6. Investing vs. Trading

While often used interchangeably, investing and trading denote two different approaches to entering and exiting positions in the stock market.

Investors generally take a long-term approach, buying shares in companies they believe in and holding on to these shares for years or even decades, disregarding the short-term market fluctuations.

On the other hand, traders attempt to profit from short-term price fluctuations and trends. They're less concerned with the fundamental value of the company and more with the movement of the stock price.

2.7. Risks Associated with Stock Markets

As rewarding as the stock market could be, it's not without risks. Market conditions can change abruptly and unexpectedly due to a wide range of factors - business cycles, interest rate changes, political events, and more.

One of the core elements of mastering the stock market is the ability to manage these risks. It involves understanding your risk tolerance, diversifying your investments, establishing a solid investment plan, and being disciplined in implementing it.

In summary, the stock market is a fascinating, complex universe, filled with opportunities. By taking the time to understand how the market works and learning how to navigate its waters, you'll equip yourself with the ability to transform your financial future. It's a journey requiring patience, education, strategy, and risk management, but the potential rewards make it all worthwhile. You're on the path to becoming masters of arguably the most powerful wealth-building tool in human history: the stock market.

Chapter 3. Demystifying Stock Market Jargon

Whether you're dipping your toes or diving headfirst into the Sea of Stocks, understanding the language is just as crucial as grasping the fundamental strategies and principles of investing. For many would-be investors, stock market jargon can seem daunting or even impenetrable. We're here to change that. So, buckle up as we break down some of the most crucial terminologies you'll encounter in your journey towards financial independence.

3.1. Understanding Basics of Stocks and Stock Market

Before venturing deep, let's form a strong foundation by understanding what 'stocks' and the 'stock market' actually means. A stock represents a share in the ownership of a company and constitutes a claim on a portion of the company's assets and earnings. The stock market, on the other hand, is a marketplace where buyers and sellers trade these stocks.

3.2. Terms Related to Stocks

Blue-Chip Stocks: These are shares in large, well-established and financially stable companies with a reliable history of performance. Think companies like Apple, Microsoft, or Coca-Cola.

Growth Stocks: These are shares in companies projected to grow at an above-average rate compared to other firms on the market.

Dividend Stocks: Companies that pay out dividends (an "extra" sum of money on top of earnings, usually quarterly) offer dividend stocks. They can provide a steady income, making them a popular choice for long-term investors.

Volume: This represents the number of shares traded during a specific period (typically a day). High trading volumes can indicate strong investor interest and are a critical factor when short-term trading.

3.3. Navigating the Stock Market Indices

An index is a benchmark or a measure of a country's economic health or its markets. Let's explore some globally recognized stock market indices.

Dow Jones Industrial Average (DJIA): This is an index that tracks the 30 large publicly-owned companies trading on the NYSE.

NASDAQ Composite: This index includes all the companies listed on the NASDAQ stock exchange, much known for technological and innovation-based enterprises.

S&P 500: An index that tracks the performance of 500 large companies listed on the US stock market.

3.4. Understanding Buyers, Sellers and Market Orders

Bid: The bid is the price a buyer is willing to pay for a security.

Ask (Offer): Conversely, the 'ask' or 'offer' is the price a seller is willing to accept for a security.

Spread: This is the difference between the bid (buy) price and ask (sell) price.

Limit Order: This is a type of order to buy or sell a stock at a specific price or better. Setting a limit order ensures that you don't pay more (or sell for less) than anticipated.

Market Order: A market order is a request by an investor to purchase or sell a security at the best available price in the current market.

Stop-Loss Order: This is an order placed to buy or sell a stock once it reaches a specific price. Investors typically use this to limit a loss or protect a profit on a stock they own.

3.5. Making Sense of the Earnings Reports and Ratios

Earnings Per Share (EPS): EPS is a portion of a company's profit allocated to each share of common stock. It serves as an indicator of a company's profitability.

Price-to-Earnings Ratio (P/E): This ratio measures the market's expectation of a company's future growth. Companies with high P/E ratios are often expected to deliver higher growth.

Dividend Yield: It's a financial ratio that shows how much a company pays out in dividends each year relative to its stock price.

3.6. Technical Analysis Terms

Bull Market: A market characterized by rising prices, optimism, investor confidence, and expectations that strong results will continue.

Bear Market: In contrast, a bear market is one where prices are falling, leading to widespread pessimism. If the decline is 20% or more, it's considered a bear market.

Volatility: It refers to the amount of uncertainty or risk related to the changes in a security's value. High volatility means that a security's value can potentially be spread out over a larger range of values.

Resistances and Supports: These are pre-determined levels of a price where it tends to stop and reverse. Resistance is a level where the price tends to find opposition as it rises, while support refers to the price level where buying is strong enough to interrupt the selling pressure.

Fear and Greed Index: This index is used by investors to gauge market sentiment. It swings along a scale of 0 to 100, indicating "extreme fear" to "extreme greed."

Understanding these terms will allow you to confidently navigate the stock market universe. As you follow this educational journey, remember that knowledge is power, especially when it comes to investing. So keep learning, keep investing, and keep growing. This concludes the chapter on "Demystifying Stock Market Jargon." Up next, we will deep-dive into the strategies for stock market success!

Chapter 4. Analyzing the Market: The Art of Making Informed Decisions

Market analysis plays a fundamental role in stock trading. To be a successful stock trader, you must understand how to analyze and interpret the financial market correctly. This chapter explores the critical aspects of market analysis, providing actionable insights to help you make informed decisions.

4.1. Understanding Market Indicators

Market indicators are statistical metrics used by traders to predict market trends. The most commonly used indicators include price, volume, volatility, momentum, and market sentiment. Each of these represents a different aspect of market behavior and, when combined, offer comprehensive insights to aid your decision-making process.

Price dictates the cost at which a stock is bought or sold. Monitoring price trends can give you an understanding of the stability or volatility of a given stock.

Volume refers to the number of shares traded during a particular period. High trading volumes typically indicate strong investor interest and can point to the start of a new trend.

Volatility measures the price fluctuations of a stock. Greater volatility often means higher risk, but it could also mean greater returns.

Momentum is a measure of the speed of a price increase or decrease for a set of shares. It helps traders understand the amount of conviction behind a trend.

Market sentiment refers to the overall attitude of investors toward a specific security or financial market. It is often used as a contrarian indicator.

4.2. Technical and Fundamental Analysis

The two primary methods of market analysis are technical analysis and fundamental analysis.

Technical Analysis is a method that involves examining past market data to predict future price movements. Technical analysts operate under the belief that all current market information is reflected in the price, making it the only data worth considering. They identify patterns or trends in price movements and use mathematical indicators to predict future activity. Some commonly used technical analysis tools include moving averages, trendlines, and momentum oscillators.

Fundamental Analysis, conversely, involves evaluating a company's intrinsic value by examining related economic and financial factors. Fundamental analysts believe that the stock market may misprice a company temporarily, but the correct price will eventually be reached. Factors such as earnings reports, balance sheets, cash flow statements, and the current economic condition are all utilized in the fundamental analytical process.

Both methods have their advantages and limitations; hence many investors tend to use a combination of both. Understanding and utilizing both techniques can greatly improve your decision-making skills.

4.3. Reading Financial Statements

A crucial part of fundamental analysis is understanding how to read and interpret a company's financial statements. These reflect a company's performance and are usually made up of the balance sheet, income statement, and cash flow statement.

The **balance sheet** provides an overview of a company's assets, liabilities, and shareholders' equity. The difference between assets and liabilities represents the net worth or equity of a company.

The **income statement** shows the company's revenues, costs, and expenses over a period. It offers a clear understanding of the company's profits and losses.

Lastly, the **cash flow statement** outlines how much cash is coming into or going out of the business. It reveals how a company raises cash for its activities and how it spends that cash.

Understanding these financial documents is key to evaluating a company's health and profitability, hence crucial to making informed investment decisions.

4.4. Risk Management

It's important to acknowledge that there are unavoidable risks involved with trading on the stock market. Risk management is a crucial aspect of successful trading. To manage your risk:

- **Diversify Your Portfolio:** Don't put all your eggs in one basket. Ensure your investments are spread across different sectors;

- **Set Stop-Loss Orders:** This allows you to set a predetermined level of loss that you're willing to take on a particular investment;

- **Adjust Positions:** Reflect on your investment strategy regularly and make adjustments as need be;

- **Invest Only What You Can Afford to Lose:** Never invest money that you cannot afford to lose, such as your emergency fund or money set aside for basic living expenses.

4.5. Conclusion

In conclusion, successful stock trading requires a blend of knowledge, skills, and strategies, chief among them being a firm grasp of market analysis. By studying market indicators, mastering technical and fundamental analysis, and understanding risk management, you set yourself on a promising path to stock market mastery.

Chapter 5. Strategies for Successful Portfolio Diversification

Portfolio diversification undeniably stands as a cornerstone for achieving long-term financial success in the stock market. However, beyond the common wisdom of "don't put all your eggs in one basket," many investors have little understanding of what diversification truly entails or how to successfully implement it. This special report will plunge you deeper into this critical principle, distilling the complex facets of diversification into comprehensible and actionable strategies.

5.1. Understanding Diversification

Diversification refers to the strategic allocation of investment holdings across different asset classes, industries, or geographical locations to reduce risk. The purpose of diversification isn't necessarily to boost performance, but rather to insulate your portfolio against severe losses.

Suppose you invest all your capital in a single stock. If that company performs well, your returns could be phenomenal. However, if that company fails, your entire investment is at risk. By owning a collection of different investments, the poor performance of a single stock is likely to be offset by the good performance of others.

5.2. The Role of Asset Allocation

Asset allocation plays a vital role in successful diversification. Depending on your age, financial goals, and risk tolerance, assets can be broadly classified into three categories: equities (stocks), fixed-income (bonds), and cash equivalents.

As a general rule, equities tend to offer higher returns but also carry higher risk. Conversely, bonds typically provide lower returns but are more stable, while cash equivalents offer the lowest risk and return. Balancing these assets is crucial. For example, a youthful investor could invest a larger portion in equities due to their high growth potential and adapt their portfolio as they age towards more bonds and cash equivalents.

5.3. Diversified Within Each Asset Type

Even within each asset type, further diversification is necessary. If investing in equities, don't invest in just one company. Ideally, you should have a mix of offerings from various industries such as technology, consumer goods, health care, finance, and others.

When it comes to bonds, diversify among corporate, municipal, and government bonds. This approach will guard your investments against downturns in a specific sector or industry, enhancing your portfolio's stability.

5.4. The Importance of Geographic Diversification

Your diversification should not be limited to industries or types of assets; geographic diversification is equally crucial. This involves spreading your investments across different countries or regions. For instance, if the U.S. market experiences a downturn, your European or Asian holdings might perform better, mitigating your overall losses.

5.5. Index Funds and ETFs: A shortcut to Diversification

A simple way to achieve broad diversification is through index funds and Exchange-Traded Funds (ETFs). These are designed to mimic the performance of a particular index, like the S&P 500, often comprising of different industries, making them inherently diversified. ETFs offer the added advantage of trading like stocks, providing flexibility for investors.

5.6. The Dangers of Overdiversification

While diversification is fundamental to risk management, there's such a thing as overdiversification. Owning too many different types of assets might make managing your portfolio overwhelming. More importantly, it could dilute your returns, as profits from well-performing investments are watered down by the sheer number of total holdings. Keeping the number of investments to a reasonable level allows you to stay informed about every holding and act promptly when necessary.

5.7. Regular Portfolio Rebalancing

Diversification isn't a "set-it-and-forget-it" strategy. Instead, it requires regular monitoring and rebalancing to maintain your chosen asset allocation. Over time, some investments will perform better than others, skewing your original asset distribution. Rebalancing these assets strategically can help maintain the desired risk-to-reward ratio.

In conclusion, successful portfolio diversification is an art perfected over time. It involves understanding your financial goals, assessing your risk tolerance, and continuously researching and rebalancing your investments. The true value of diversification doesn't lie in guaranteeing profits, but rather in mitigating risks and smoothing the financial journey to your goals.

Chapter 6. Timing the Market Versus Time in the Market: What You Really Need to Know

Investing in the stock market has always been a matter of precision, strategy, and most importantly, patience. Two of the many strategies that investors often wrestle with are 'Timing the Market' and 'Time in the Market.' This debate embodies the principle conflict of investment strategy: active versus passive investing. By understanding these strategies, you'll have a key to unlocking a potentially prosperous future. With each section, we will unveil practical knowledge that can help you navigate these turbulent investment seas.

6.1. Understanding Market Timing

First, let's delve into the concept of "market timing." This strategy involves making investing decisions based on expected future price movements. Using this approach, an investor tries to predict the future direction of the market, or a particular stock, aiming to buy at the lowest point and sell at the highest. Market timing relies heavily on analysis and prediction, and is often based on technical analysis, economic data, and market research.

Proponents of timing the market argue that smart, tactical investment choices can lead to greater profit. They point to moments of extreme market volatility as opportunities to make significant gains, outperforming the market over time.

However, the biggest downside to market timing is the inherent unpredictability of markets. Despite the most careful analysis and prediction, markets can and do behave in unexpected ways. Trying to time the market can lead to stress, costly mistakes, and potential losses.

Moreover, evidence shows that even seasoned professionals often fail at predicting the market consistently. Short-term fluctuations are largely unpredictable, and the costs of being wrong can be severe. This evidence has caused even the staunchest advocates to question the efficacy and wisdom of a 'timing-the-market' approach.

6.2. The Power of Time in the Market

Now, let's explore the other side of the debate: the 'Time in the Market' philosophy. This passive investment strategy involves buying and holding investments for a long period, regardless of fluctuations in the market. Investors who employ this strategy believe in the long-term potential growth of the market, resisting the urge to react or predict short-term market movements.

The primary benefit of this approach is its simplicity. Instead of trying to predict market movements, investors can put their energies into choosing solid investments and holding them over time. This allows the power of compounding to work in their favor, as profits earned are reinvested to generate additional earnings over time.

Another benefit of time in the market is the reduction of risk. By smoothing out the impact of short-term volatility and price fluctuations, long-term investing allows the investor to ride out downturns and capitalize on upward trends in the market.

6.3. Market Timing Versus Time in the Market

From our understanding of both principles, we observe that both strategies stem from different philosophies and carry unique risks and rewards. Choosing between these two approaches often depends on an investor's financial goals, risk tolerance, and investment timeline.

It's crucial to remember that while market timing requires a proactive approach and could potentially offer significant returns, it requires a deep understanding of market trends and entails substantial risks. On the other hand, time in the market is a passive and potentially safer strategy, allowing investors to reap the benefits of long-term market growth and compounding returns.

6.4. Verdict: Which Strategy Wins?

Investment strategy should always hinge on personal factors such as risk tolerance, time horizon, and investment knowledge. That said, for most ordinary investors, a 'time in the market' approach may be the most prudent path to follow. The passive long-term investment approach not only reduces stress but also decreases trading costs, and has generally proven to be more successful over the long term. This is not to say that market timing can't be successful, but the risk, effort, and skill involved make it a less optimal strategy for most individuals.

6.5. Wrapping Up

Remember, stock market investing is no exact science. While 'Time in the Market' typically offers a more risk-averse, steady path to financial growth, 'Market Timing' does present opportunities for significant gains. It's up to each investor to decide which strategy aligns better with their financial goals and comfort level with risk. Do your homework, assess your position, and make an informed decision. Wealth building is indeed a marathon, not a sprint – it requires both tenacity and patience in ample measure.

By uncovering the nuances of both these strategies, we hope to have helped you make an informed and confident foray into your journey of stock market mastery. Remain steadfast in your quest. The road may seem daunting, but remember, with knowledge comes power, and with power, comes the ability to make effective decisions in your path towards financial independence and prosperity.

Chapter 7. Protecting Your Investments: Risk Management Techniques

In investment circles, it's well agreed that 'not losing money' is paramount to building wealth over time. You could have the best investment strategy in the world, but if you sidestep risk management, you're likely to find yourself making unplanned exits in market crashes and recessions. Follow through as we dissect risk management techniques that could be your shield against adverse market conditions.

7.1. Understanding Risk

Risk, in financial terms, is the chance that an investment's actual return will differ from the expected. This can include the potential loss of your original investment or potential for a lower than expected return. Various types of risks include Market Risk, Credit Risk, Liquidity Risk, Operational Risk, and Legal Risk. Market Risk and Credit Risk are the most pertinent to stock market investors. Knowledge about these nuances often distinguishes a savvy investor from an average one.

To manage risk, it's important to first understand your risk tolerance. Risk tolerance refers to the amount of risk you're comfortable taking. It depends on various factors like your financial situation, investment goals, time horizon, etc. Only invest within the parameters of your risk tolerance and keep revising it as situations change.

7.2. Effective Diversification

One of the simplest and most effective risk management techniques is diversification. This involves spreading your investments across various assets so that you're not overly dependent on a single investment or sector. In case a particular stock or sector performs poorly, your losses are minimized by gains in other areas.

Diversification isn't just about investing in different companies; it involves investing in companies across different sectors, geographical locations, and even asset classes. A portfolio diversified in this way is equipped to weather various economic conditions.

7.3. Regular Portfolio Rebalancing

Over time, due to varying growth rates of investments, your portfolio may disproportionately favor a particular asset class or industry. To maintain the desired level of risk, you need regular rebalancing. Rebalancing involves selling over-performing assets and buying under-performing ones to maintain the initial asset allocation.

Rebalancing not only keeps your portfolio in check but also helps in maintaining your desired risk levels and can also lead to buying low and selling high, naturally.

7.4. Use of Stop Loss Orders

Stop-loss orders are a specific type of order you can place with your broker. It sells an asset when it reaches a particular price point. By doing so, it can limit an investor's loss on a security position.

For instance, if you buy a stock at $50 and place a stop loss order for $45, the stock will be sold as soon as the price drops to $45, preventing any further loss. This technique protects your investment, but be cautious not to set your stop loss too close to your buying price, as normal market volatility might cause a premature sell off.

7.5. Hedging

Hedging is an advanced risk management technique that involves using financial instruments, typically derivatives, to offset potential losses from an investment. A popular method is buying opposite (sell/short) positions in related securities. The gain one derives from these will typically offset losses incurred from the original asset.

While hedging offers protection from adverse market movements, its implementation might be complex for novice investors. It's also important to remember that while hedging reduces risk, it also eats into potential profits.

7.6. Due Diligence

The importance of conducting thorough research before investing cannot be overstressed. Understand a company's fundamentals, management team, business model and industry outlook. Also, follow news about your investments and wider market indicators for potential challenges or opportunities. Regularly vet your portfolio for signs of risk.

Risk management is an essential part of your investment journey. It's true that risks and rewards go hand in hand, but managing those risks intelligently can make the path to stock market mastery smoother and more predictable. With these strategies under your belt, you are equipped to secure your investments, allowing your wealth to consistently grow. Stick diligently to these principles, always be willing to learn new techniques, and keep abreast of the latest market trends. Before long, you'll be well on your way to achieving financial independence and a comfortable future.

Chapter 8. Bull vs. Bear: Thriving in Various Market Conditions

Understanding the varying market conditions, represented by the Bull and the Bear market scenarios, is a key aspect of mastering the stock market. Grasping the dynamics of these market states and learning how to thrive in each, sets a discerning investor a cut above the rest. Let's delve into the depths of what these market conditions mean and how you can navigate them.

8.1. The Bull Market

A bull market is characterized by a sustained period of rising asset prices, fueled by investor confidence, optimism, and positive market sentiment. It generally happens during times of strong gross domestic product (GDP) growth and falling unemployment, and the market trend is predominantly upwards.

1. **Understanding the Bull:** In a bull market, investors are willing to take more risks as the overall economic outlook is robust, and companies report higher earnings. With the surge in optimism, the demand for stocks exceeds the supply, leading to an incessant rise in share prices. A bull market typically lasts for several months, sometimes even years.

2. **Thriving in a Bull Market:** Making the most of a bull market starts with an investment strategy that can capitalize on rising stock prices. Some strategies that could be potentially rewarding include 'buy and hold,' 'growth investing,' and 'momentum investing.'

In a 'buy and hold' strategy, you buy stocks when the prices are relatively low, and hold on to them throughout the market upswing, selling only when the market reaches its peak. 'Growth investing' involves investing in companies that are expected to grow at an above-average rate compared to other stocks, typically new companies in innovative industries.

'Momentum investing,' on the other hand, involves investing in trending stocks that have shown significant price changes over the last few months, capitalizing on the ongoing market trends.

Of course, while the prices are generally upward-trending, remember, not all stocks will rise during a bull market. Hence, it's crucial to diversify your portfolio, do your research, and make informed decisions.

8.2. The Bear Market

A Bear market is the polar opposite of its Bull counterpart. It represents a prolonged period of falling stock prices, often accompanied by negative investor sentiment, pessimism, and economic slowdown. It's generally precipitated by weakening GDP growth, rising unemployment, and several other economic factors.

1. **Understanding the Bear:** In a bear market, investors are generally nervous and reluctant to invest as companies start to report declining earnings, leading to a decrease in stock prices. As the pessimism becomes widespread, selling becomes more prevalent than buying, pushing share prices lower and prolonging the bear market phase.

2. **Thriving in a Bear Market:** Surviving and even thriving during a bear market is possible, albeit somewhat more challenging. This phase calls for strategies like 'short selling,' 'defensive investing,' and the use of 'stop-loss orders.'

'Short selling,' also known as shorting, involves borrowing shares to sell them at a higher price, then repurchasing them when the price drops, pocketing the difference. 'Defensive investing' involves taking positions in stable 'defensive' stocks—those of companies whose goods and services are always in demand, regardless of the economic situation.

'Stop-loss orders' are tools that can protect your portfolio from significant losses. Setting a stop-loss order for a stock will automatically sell it once the price drops to a predetermined level, thus preventing drastic losses.

While adopting these techniques, always remember that bear markets are temporary, and the downturn will eventually give way to a new bull market. Hence, consider bear markets as potential opportunities to buy quality stocks at lower prices, in anticipation of future gains.

8.3. Adapting to Market Conditions

The stock market is ever-evolving, and mastering it involves adapting your strategy to not only survive but thrive under changing conditions. This means staying informed about global economic trends, continually learning about various investment vehicles, conducting solid research, and keeping your emotions in check to avoid making rash decisions.

Knowing how to handle both bull and bear markets is a step towards becoming a well-rounded investor. The objective isn't just to chase quick profits during bullish times but to position your portfolio for long-term success, weathering any storms that come your way.

8.4. Managing Fear and Greed

The two dominant emotions governing investor behavior are fear and greed. During bull markets, investors can be overwhelmed by greed, driving them to push beyond their risk limits. Conversely, fear can dominate during bear markets, leading to panic selling. Managing these emotions is critical in mastering the stock market.

Try developing a disciplined investment plan that aligns with your risk tolerance and investment goals. Avoid getting carried away by short-term market trends and always keep your long-term financial objectives in view. Having this stable strategic foundation adds rationality to your decisions, mitigating the influence of fear and greed.

8.5. Conclusion

Successful stock market investing isn't about fearing bear markets or getting carried away with bull markets. It's about understanding these market conditions, adapting your strategies accordingly, and making informed decisions. The real secret of wealth-building lies within this crucial equilibrium of understanding and execution.

Cracking the code of the bull and bear markets is undoubtedly an essential aspect of mastering the stock market. Armed with this knowledge, you're well on your way to making smart investment decisions, irrespective of the market condition, and inching closer to your dream of financial independence.

Chapter 9. Dividends: The Power of Passive Income

In a world where fast-paced growth stocks and high-risk investments often command the spotlight, dividends—while not as glamorous—often form the stability that investors need in their portfolios to build wealth. In fact, dividends have the potential to contribute a significant portion of overall returns in the long run. But what are dividends, exactly? And how can they be leveraged to provide passive income?

First, let's define dividends. When companies generate profits, they have a few choices. They can reinvest profits back into the business, they can acquire other companies, or they can pay out some of it back to their shareholders in the form of dividends. By owning dividend-paying stocks, investors get a share of the company's profits.

9.1. The Mechanics of Dividends

When a company decides to pay dividends, it declares the payment on a per-share basis. For instance, if you own 100 shares of a company that pays a dividend of $2 per share, you'll receive a total of $200. This capital can be reinvested or spent according to your needs.

Payment of dividends can occur at various frequencies depending on the company's policies—most commonly quarterly, but also monthly, semi-annually, or even annually. Holding shares in a variety of companies that distribute dividends at different times can provide a steady stream of income.

Dividends are generally denoted as a yield, represented as a percentage of the current share price. For instance, a company trading at $20 per share that pays a $1 dividend annually has a yield of 5%. Dividend yield helps you compare the profitability of different dividend stocks.

9.2. The Power of Reinvestment

Investors have the opportunity to reinvest dividends back into the stock through a method known as Dividend Reinvestment Plans (DRIPs). By doing so, you purchase more shares with your dividend money, which, in turn, would earn even more dividends. This phenomenon, known as compound interest, can significantly increase your total returns over a long time horizon. It's a simple, yet powerful way to amplify your wealth gradually.

Consider this: if a company offers a 4% dividend yield and you reinvest this dividend, presuming the price of the stock continues to grow at the historical average rate of 7% per year, then your effective return will be more than 11% per year.

9.3. Dividend Aristocrats: A Class Apart

There's a unique class of dividend-paying stocks known as Dividend Aristocrats. These are companies in the S&P 500 index that have not only paid but also increased their dividend for at least 25 consecutive years. They provide a unique mix of growth and income potential.

By consistently increasing their dividend, these companies signal a strong financial health and a commitment to returning profits back to shareholders. Over time, an increasing dividend, when reinvested, can snowball into significant wealth.

9.4. Risks Involved and Mitigation

Like all aspects of investing, dividend income carries risks.

Companies may reduce or even eliminate their dividends if they face financial difficulties. A heavy dividend-focused strategy could also limit capital appreciation if a more significant proportion of a company's profits are distributed rather than being reinvested for growth.

To mitigate these risks, diversification is key. Spread investments across a variety of sectors and companies. Also, be alert to companies that pay extraordinarily high dividends—they might do so at the expense of their financial health.

9.5. Dividend Funds: A Simplified Approach

For those less inclined towards picking individual stocks, Exchange Traded Funds (ETFs) or mutual funds that focus on dividends can be a great option. These funds compile a diverse basket of dividend-paying stocks, providing instant diversification and exposure to a wide range of sectors.

9.6. Conclusion

In closing, dividends can act as a steady, reliable component of your overall investment strategy. Through the power of compounding, even a moderate yield can escalate into a substantial corpus over the long term.

No matter what your investment goals are, understanding dividends and their benefits can offer a foundation upon which you can build a fortuitous financial future. Indeed, with diligent attention to dividend yields, payout dates, and faithful reinvestment, you could build a stream of income that can support you in your quest for financial freedom.

With the right approach to dividends, the world of passive income becomes less a dream and more an achievable reality. The path to building wealth lies ahead. Now, it's yours to take.

Chapter 10. The World of ETFs, Mutual Funds, and Index Funds: Which is Right for You?

In this omnipresent financial maze, Exchange Traded Funds (ETFs), Mutual Funds, and Index Funds are three common investment vehicles that have shaped the fortunes for millions of investors globally. By understanding their distinctive features, benefits, and shortcomings, you can make a learned decision about which is best suited for your financial goals and risk tolerance. We'll start with a precise definition followed by a comparison, then submerge into the benefits and drawbacks of each.

An Exchange Traded Fund (ETF) could be seen as a basket of securities - such as stocks, bonds, or commodities, which tracks a specific index but is traded on the stock exchange like individual stocks. Mutual Funds are investment vehicles managed by professional fund managers, pooling money from various investors to construct a diversified portfolio. Index Funds belong to the mutual fund family but with a slight twist - they passively mimic the performance of a specific index.

10.1. Understanding Exchange Traded Funds (ETFs)

ETFs amalgamate the investment scope of mutual funds with the trading flexibility of individual securities. Unlike mutual funds, ETFs are traded on an exchange, which means their price fluctuates throughout the trading day, significantly based on supply and demand.

One of the unique selling propositions of an ETF is its tax efficiency, attributed to the unique 'in-kind' creation and redemption process. This process often prevents triggering a taxable capital gain event, unlike mutual funds.

The choosing of an ETF depends on factors such as the underlying index it represents, the expense ratio, liquidity, tracking error, and the issuing institution's credibility.

10.2. Understanding Mutual Funds

A mutual fund pools money from multiple investors to invest in a diversified portfolio of stocks, bonds, or other assets, managed by professional portfolio managers. Unlike ETFs, the price of mutual funds i.e., Net Asset Value (NAV), is determined once at the end of the trading day.

Investing in mutual funds could provide simplicity and diversification at a low investment threshold. Plus, the expertise of professional managers who make investment decisions backed by comprehensive research.

However, mutual funds often come with a higher expense ratio due to active management and may result in more capital gains tax compared to ETFs or Index Funds.

10.3. Diving into Index Funds

An index fund operates under the umbrella of mutual funds but with an aim to replicate the performance of a specific index, such as the S&P 500. Because of their passive nature, index funds typically come with low expense ratios and turnover rates.

Investors choosing index funds gain exposure to a wide variety of securities, thereby ensuring diversification and mitigating the risk associated with single security investing. These funds are perfect for individuals who believe in the prowess of market efficiency and prefer a buy-and-hold strategy.

10.4. Which is Right for You?

Choosing between an ETF, mutual fund, or an index fund depends on factors such as investment goals, risk tolerance, cost sensitivity, investment amount, and your preference for active or passive investing.

ETFs could be the right choice for investors seeking high flexibility, tax efficiency, and the possibility of tactical asset allocation. Meanwhile, mutual funds might be more suitable for those who prefer professional management of their investment and are comfortable with a slightly higher cost.

For believers of market efficiency and the power of passive investing, index funds can be an excellent choice. They offer broad market exposure that results in low risk, and their low expense ratios make them a cost-effective investment option.

In conclusion, financial success in the stock market doesn't always come from picking the highest performing stocks. Often, it comes from understanding different investment options, aligning them with your financial aspirations, and persisting with disciplined investing. ETFs, mutual funds, and index funds each have their respective advantages and disadvantages. As an investor, the key lies in understanding which option aligns most closely with your investment strategy and objectives while considering the balance between risk and rewards.

Chapter 11. Planning for the Future: Retirement and Beyond

The journey to financial independence begins with planning, envisioning the kind of future you want, and how you can get there. In the world of investing, this is particularly important as the decisions you make today can significantly impact your wealth and lifestyle tomorrow.

Retirement might seem far off, but it's never too early to put measures in place to ensure you live comfortably in the autumn of your life and even beyond.

11.1. The Principles of Retirement Planning

Retirement planning, at its core, involves figuring out your retirement goals and the actions you'll need to take to reach them. This takes into consideration your present income, your savings rate, your expected retirement age, and the lifestyle you envision.

Your retirement fund will be influenced dramatically by the amount of time you have to invest. The earlier you start, the better your potential returns due to the power of compounding. Remember that every bit counts, and even modest investments can grow significantly over decades.

Aside from income and savings, your investment strategy plays an integral role in retirement planning. Strategic diversification and a balanced portfolio can help insulate you from market fluctuations and ensure steady growth over time.

11.2. Assessing Your Retirement Needs

To start with, you'll need to have a clear picture of what your retired life would look like — this could include traveling, starting a business, or helping grandchildren pay for their university fees. With a clearly defined goal, you can then determine the amount of saving required. Factor in inflation and potential medical costs, which can be substantial in later years.

If your annual income is $75,000 and you expect to live comfortably on 80% of this figure in retirement ($60,000), your target savings should be roughly 25 times your expected annual expenses, or about $1.5 million considering the 4% safe withdrawal rate rule.

11.3. Saving and Investment Strategies

Start saving early and regularly. A common mistake that most people make is waiting too late in their career to start actively saving for retirement. The earlier you start, the longer your savings have to grow thanks to the beauty of compound interest.

In terms of where to invest your savings, diversification across various asset classes is crucial. A well-diversified portfolio can withstand market volatility and potentially offer more consistent returns. Equities, bonds, and real estate are popular investment categories that should be part of any long-term strategy.

Online tools like brokerage calculators or robo-advisors can help you automate your investment strategy. They can help you determine your risk tolerance and suggest an investment strategy accordingly.

11.4. Understanding Social Security

In addition to your personal savings and investments, social security benefits are an important part of your retirement strategy. The benefits you can receive depend on your 35 highest-earning years and your age when you start receiving benefits.

Starting your social security benefits at your full retirement age (which is typically between 66 - 67) will get you 100% benefits based on your earnings history. But if you can delay, you'd receive a bonus amount for every year until age 70.

11.5. Estate Planning Beyond Retirement

Finally, as you plan for retirement, it's also vital to consider what you'll leave behind. Estate planning helps to ensure your assets go to the right beneficiaries with minimal erosion from tax liabilities.

Include all your assets in your estate — real estate, investments, business interests, and even personal items. Consider setting up a trust to manage your assets when you're gone, particularly if your estate is large, and consider discussing your plans with your family to avoid potential disputes in the future.

11.6. Conclusion

Planning for retirement is as much about your lifestyle and ambitions as it is about numbers and finances. With the correct approach, a well thought-out plan can help you secure a prosperous post-retirement life for you and your loved ones and ensure you leave the right legacy. Remember, it's never too early or too late to begin this journey, and the bedrock of this effort is robust financial education. Let your pursuit to wealth and prosperity in your golden years begin today!

www.ingramcontent.com/pod-product-compliance
Lightning Source LLC
Chambersburg PA
CBHW071049260726
48661CB00007B/3219